# Wilson Fluency® / Basic

## Reader Two

Closed Syllables (Blends / Welded Sounds)

**FIRST EDITION**

WILSON LANGUAGE TRAINING CORPORATION

**www.wilsonlanguage.com**

# Wilson Fluency® / Basic • Reader 2

Item # WFBR2

ISBN 978-1-56778-317-9
FIRST EDITION

PUBLISHED BY:

**Wilson Language Training Corporation**
47 Old Webster Road
Oxford, MA 01540
United States of America

(800) 899-8454

www.wilsonlanguage.com

Printed in the U.S.A.
November 2013

**2**

# WILSON Fluency®
## Reader Two

WILSON®

STUDENT NAME

# Wilson Fluency® / Basic · Reader 2

**Hank (2.1)**

# Chart your progress from drill to drill!

Mark your scores at top of each chart.

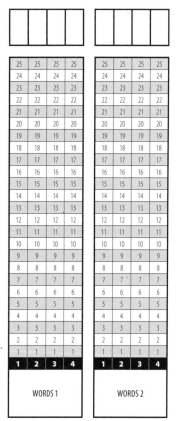

| WORDS 1 | WORDS 2 | PHRASES 1 | PHRASES 2 | BASELINE | PHRASED READING | UN-PHRASED READING |
|---|---|---|---|---|---|---|
| 1 2 3 4 | 1 2 3 4 | 1 2 3 4 | 1 2 3 4 | 1 | 1 2 | 1 2 |

**Hank**

| | | | | |
|---|---|---|---|---|
| Hank | bank | junk | tank | long |
| thanks | song | think | things | sink |
| pink | cans | shack | cash | song |
| gas | things | man | luck | hill |
| sang | sell | caps | shells | job |

WORDS 2

| | | | | |
|---|---|---|---|---|
| who | new | one | some | now |
| have | his | would | day | new |
| for | could | was | and | to |
| the | his | some | do | a |
| what | he | you | of | said |

was a man

in the bank

did not think

some hub caps

had tin cans

a sink to sell

Hank hung up

the pink shells

had no cash

a junk box

in the tank

this sad song

think that things

for his junk

lug his things

was one of thanks

had no gas in the tank

would get much better

got him some cash too

could sell his things there

who was down on his luck

met his friend Ben

no longer a sad one

he also had tin cans

Hank hung up "For Sale"

sad song did not help

# Hank

Hank was a man who was down on his luck. He had no cash in the bank. Hank had a van but it was not a new one at all. It was a junk box! It did get him to his job, but now he had no gas in the tank and no cash to get the gas. All day long, Hank sang a sad song. He did not think that things would get much better. This sad song did not help him.

Then he met his friend Ben. Ben said that a sad song would not help him at all. He said that Hank should sell things to get some cash for gas. "What do you have that you can sell?" asked Ben. Hank had some hub caps and a sink to sell. He also had tin cans with pink shells in them.

Ben had a shack and said that Hank could sell his things there. Hank hung up "For Sale" and set up his shop. He had to lug his things up the hill to the shack and it was a big job.

Hank did not think that he could get cash for his junk, but he did! He got a lot of cash for the sink and the hub caps, and the pink shells got him some cash too.

Now Hank could get some gas and get to his job. His song was no longer a sad one, it was one of thanks.

# Hank

Hank was a man who was down on his luck. He had
no cash in the bank. Hank had a van but it was not a new
one at all. It was a junk box! It did get him to his job, but
now he had no gas in the tank and no cash to get the gas.
All day long, Hank sang a sad song. He did not think that
things would get much better. This sad song did not help
him.

Then he met his friend Ben. Ben said that a sad song
would not help him at all. He said that Hank should sell
things to get some cash for gas. "What do you have that

you can sell?" asked Ben. Hank had some hub caps and a sink to sell. He also had tin cans with pink shells in them.

Ben had a shack and said that Hank could sell his things there. Hank hung up "For Sale" and set up his shop. He had to lug his things up the hill to the shack and it was a big job.

Hank did not think that he could get cash for his junk, but he did! He got a lot of cash for the sink and the hub caps, and the pink shells got him some cash too.

Now Hank could get some gas and get to his job. His song was no longer a sad one, it was one of thanks.

# Chart your progress from drill to drill!

Mark your scores at top of each chart.

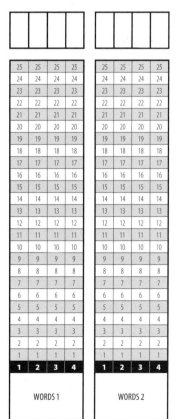

**Fish in Small Pond (2.2)**

| WORDS 1 | WORDS 2 | PHRASES 1 | PHRASES 2 | BASELINE | PHRASED READING | UN-PHRASED READING |
|---------|---------|-----------|-----------|----------|-----------------|--------------------|

# Fish in Small Pond

| | | | | |
|---|---|---|---|---|
| bench | pond | glad | spot | sand |
| best | steps | went | rest | spin |
| cast | felt | stop | jump | trip |
| hand | small | last | Stan | end |
| swim | clock | still | bend | black |

WORDS 2

| | | | | |
|---|---|---|---|---|
| want | they | been | other | one |
| two | from | could | first | was |
| about | and | day | some | the |
| could | new | he | of | been |
| they | other | his | a | to |

| | |
|---|---|
| Stan got up | he was glad |
| on a trip | was ten steps |
| from a bench | but at first |
| Stan could sit | he felt sad |
| had to stop | in his hand |
| the best one | cast his rod |
| the wet sand | in the end |
| back to Small Pond | he got not one |

**Fish in Small Pond**

to rest on the bench

did it again and again

with Josh last summer

on a trip with his friend

but Stan did not think

was full of big fish

his best day fishing ever

all in the same spot

glad it was here at last

stood on wet sand

# Fish in Small Pond

It was six o'clock and Stan got up. This was a big day and he did not want to miss it. He was glad it was here at last. Stan was going on a trip with his friend, Josh, and Josh's dad, back to Small Pond. It was called Small Pond, but Stan did not think that it was small at all. It was too big to swim across it.

Stan had been to Small Pond with Josh last summer. The pond was full of big fish. He had so much luck that other time with his black rod. That time, he got not one - not two - but six fish, all in the same spot! It had been his best day fishing ever.

When they got to Small Pond, they went back to that spot. It was ten steps from a bench and so Stan could sit on it to rest. But at first, he stood on the wet sand and cast his rod. He did it again and again. No luck! He felt sad but he did not stop. Still, he had no luck.

At last, Stan had to stop to rest on the bench. He set his rod in the wet sand. Just as he sat, he saw his rod bend and spin and he jumped to get it. It was back in his hand. He was in luck. This fish was huge! In the end, Stan just had one fish, but it was the best one.

# Fish in Small Pond

It was six o'clock and Stan got up. This was a big day and he did not want to miss it. He was glad it was here at last. Stan was going on a trip with his friend, Josh, and Josh's dad, back to Small Pond. It was called Small Pond, but Stan did not think that it was small at all. It was too big to swim across it.

Stan had been to Small Pond with Josh last summer. The pond was full of big fish. He had so much luck that other time with his black rod. That time, he got not one - not two - but six fish, all in the same spot! It had been his best day fishing ever.

When they got to Small Pond, they went back to that spot. It was ten steps from a bench and so Stan could sit on it to rest. But at first, he stood on the wet sand and cast his rod. He did it again and again. No luck! He felt sad but he did not stop. Still, he had no luck.

At last, Stan had to stop to rest on the bench. He set his rod in the wet sand. Just as he sat, he saw his rod bend and spin and he jumped to get it. It was back in his hand. He was in luck. This fish was huge! In the end, Stan just had one fish, but it was the best one.

# Chart your progress from drill to drill!

Mark your scores at top of each chart.

| | | | |
|---|---|---|---|
| 25 | 25 | 25 | 25 |
| 24 | 24 | 24 | 24 |
| 23 | 23 | 23 | 23 |
| 22 | 22 | 22 | 22 |
| 21 | 21 | 21 | 21 |
| 20 | 20 | 20 | 20 |
| 19 | 19 | 19 | 19 |
| 18 | 18 | 18 | 18 |
| 17 | 17 | 17 | 17 |
| 16 | 16 | 16 | 16 |
| 15 | 15 | 15 | 15 |
| 14 | 14 | 14 | 14 |
| 13 | 13 | 13 | 13 |
| 12 | 12 | 12 | 12 |
| 11 | 11 | 11 | 11 |
| 10 | 10 | 10 | 10 |
| 9 | 9 | 9 | 9 |
| 8 | 8 | 8 | 8 |
| 7 | 7 | 7 | 7 |
| 6 | 6 | 6 | 6 |
| 5 | 5 | 5 | 5 |
| 4 | 4 | 4 | 4 |
| 3 | 3 | 3 | 3 |
| 2 | 2 | 2 | 2 |
| 1 | 1 | 1 | 1 |
| **1** | **2** | **3** | **4** |

WORDS 1

WORDS 2

PHRASES 1

PHRASES 2

BASELINE

PHRASED READING

UN-PHRASED READING

| | | | | |
|---|---|---|---|---|
| gold | cold | most | old | kind |
| things | went | punch | Smith | kept |
| find | sift | fact | rocks | sold |
| stop | sand | chunk | swish | glad |
| luck | rush | left | last | long |

**STORY 3**

WORDS 2

| | | | | |
|---|---|---|---|---|
| out | into | one | any | put |
| first | they | would | into | who |
| put | water | was | one | by |
| he | and | for | day | the |
| to | some | be | a | his |

| | |
|---|---|
| sand went out | lots of them |
| they would sift | to find gold |
| one big chunk | put the pan |
| kind old man | into the cold |
| most men left | sift the sand |
| big old bag | did not find |
| left with gold | did not stop |
| small rocks and gold | most gold of all |

for a long time                    men went to Cold Creek

would first punch small holes      pan into the cold water

went out of the holes              no gold in Cold Creek

but he kept one big chunk          by swishing the pan

but some people had luck           in the bottom of the pan

STORY 3

# Gold at Cold Creek

In the old days of the Gold Rush, many men went to Cold Creek to find gold, and lots of them did.

To find gold, people would first punch small holes in the bottom of a pan. Then they put the pan into the water to fill it with sand. They would sift the sand by swishing the pan. The sand went out of the holes, but things such as small rocks and gold did not. They would then get rid of the rocks and if they had luck, they would be left with gold in the pan! Some people did not find a thing, but some people had luck.

One of the men who went to Cold Creek was Jed Smith. He was a kind old man. Day after day, Jed went and bent over Cold Creek with a pan. All day long, he would put his pan into the cold water and sift the sand.

Then one day, there was no gold in Cold Creek. Men kept sifting the sand, but they did not find any gold. Most men left, but Jed did not stop. When he did not find gold for a long time, he too did stop at last.

In the end, Jed had lots of gold in his big old bag. In fact, he had the most gold of all. The old man sold all of his gold but he kept one big chunk of it. He was glad that he went to Cold Creek.

# Gold at Cold Creek

In the old days of the Gold Rush, many men went to Cold Creek to find gold, and lots of them did.

To find gold, people would first punch small holes in the bottom of a pan. Then they put the pan into the water to fill it with sand. They would sift the sand by swishing the pan. The sand went out of the holes, but things such as small rocks and gold did not. They would then get rid of the rocks and if they had luck, they would be left with gold in the pan! Some people did not find a thing, but some people had luck.

One of the men who went to Cold Creek was Jed Smith. He was a kind old man. Day after day, Jed went and bent over Cold Creek with a pan. All day long, he would put his pan into the cold water and sift the sand.

Then one day, there was no gold in Cold Creek. Men kept sifting the sand, but they did not find any gold. Most men left, but Jed did not stop. When he did not find gold for a long time, he too did stop at last.

In the end, Jed had lots of gold in his big old bag. In fact, he had the most gold of all. The old man sold all of his gold but he kept one big chunk of it. He was glad that he went to Cold Creek.

STORY 3

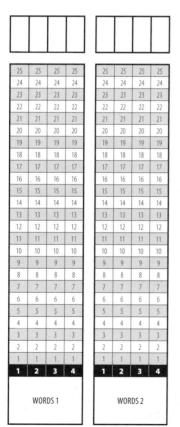

# Chart your progress from drill to drill!

Mark your scores at top of each chart.

Grump (2.4)

| WORDS 1 | WORDS 2 | PHRASES 1 | PHRASES 2 | BASELINE | PHRASED READING | UN-PHRASED READING |
|---|---|---|---|---|---|---|

| | | | | |
|---|---|---|---|---|
| Frank | blast | slept | felt | drank |
| Grump | crept | smell | skunk | just |
| slept | cold | flash | Grump | stunk |
| last | steps | chunk | black | wind |
| think | hunt | left | cold | find |

WORDS 2

| | | | | |
|---|---|---|---|---|
| two | could | one | now | by |
| been | want | into | very | for |
| about | could | out | or | would |
| some | from | put | was | of |
| first | he | and | his | be |

STORY 4

his pet dog

in his bed

he just crept

an old dog

drank some milk

Frank felt sad

of cold wind

to go out

by a skunk

a bad smell

and he stunk

Frank had to call

did not think

put Grump out

had been hit

felt sad for Grump

to hunt to get a flashlight

crept under his blanket

went into the back yard

and very sad for himself

a blast of cold wind

was coming from the shed

still did not come back

a soft whimper out back

bed since about ten o'clock

before he went to bed

# Grump

It was two a.m. and Frank had been in his bed since about ten o'clock. His pet dog, Grump, slept on his bed with him. Grump was an old dog. Just before he went to bed, Grump drank some milk and now he had to go out. Frank did not want to get up at all. At first, he just crept under his blanket. But at last, he got up to put Grump out. Grump went into the back yard.

Grump was not fast, but when he did not come back, Frank had to call him. Grump still did not come back. Next, there was a blast of cold wind. In the wind, there was a bad smell. In fact, it was a very bad smell!

Could that stink be the smell of a skunk? At first, Frank did not think so, or rather, he did not want to think so. Frank had to hunt to get a flashlight to go out to find Grump. There was one on the desk, so he went out into the black night. It was cold! There was a soft whimper out back. Could that be Grump? The whimper was coming from the shed.

Yes – it was Grump on the steps of the shed. Yes, Grump had been hit by a skunk and he stunk! It would be Frank's job to give Grump a bath. Frank felt sad for Grump and very sad for himself.

# Grump

It was two a.m. and Frank had been in his bed since about ten o'clock. His pet dog, Grump, slept on his bed with him. Grump was an old dog. Just before he went to bed, Grump drank some milk and now he had to go out. Frank did not want to get up at all. At first, he just crept under his blanket. But at last, he got up to put Grump out. Grump went into the back yard.

Grump was not fast, but when he did not come back, Frank had to call him. Grump still did not come back. Next, there was a blast of cold wind. In the wind, there was a bad smell. In fact, it was a very bad smell!

Could that stink be the smell of a skunk? At first, Frank did not think so, or rather, he did not want to think so. Frank had to hunt to get a flashlight to go out to find Grump. There was one on the desk, so he went out into the black night. It was cold! There was a soft whimper out back. Could that be Grump? The whimper was coming from the shed.

Yes – it was Grump on the steps of the shed. Yes, Grump had been hit by a skunk and he stunk! It would be Frank's job to give Grump a bath. Frank felt sad for Grump and very sad for himself.

Split Cliffs Hike (2.5)

# Chart your progress from drill to drill!

Mark your scores at top of each chart.

| WORDS 1 (1) | WORDS 1 (2) | WORDS 1 (3) | WORDS 1 (4) | WORDS 2 (1) | WORDS 2 (2) | WORDS 2 (3) | WORDS 2 (4) |
|---|---|---|---|---|---|---|---|
| 25 | 25 | 25 | 25 | 25 | 25 | 25 | 25 |
| 24 | 24 | 24 | 24 | 24 | 24 | 24 | 24 |
| 23 | 23 | 23 | 23 | 23 | 23 | 23 | 23 |
| 22 | 22 | 22 | 22 | 22 | 22 | 22 | 22 |
| 21 | 21 | 21 | 21 | 21 | 21 | 21 | 21 |
| 20 | 20 | 20 | 20 | 20 | 20 | 20 | 20 |
| 19 | 19 | 19 | 19 | 19 | 19 | 19 | 19 |
| 18 | 18 | 18 | 18 | 18 | 18 | 18 | 18 |
| 17 | 17 | 17 | 17 | 17 | 17 | 17 | 17 |
| 16 | 16 | 16 | 16 | 16 | 16 | 16 | 16 |
| 15 | 15 | 15 | 15 | 15 | 15 | 15 | 15 |
| 14 | 14 | 14 | 14 | 14 | 14 | 14 | 14 |
| 13 | 13 | 13 | 13 | 13 | 13 | 13 | 13 |
| 12 | 12 | 12 | 12 | 12 | 12 | 12 | 12 |
| 11 | 11 | 11 | 11 | 11 | 11 | 11 | 11 |
| 10 | 10 | 10 | 10 | 10 | 10 | 10 | 10 |
| 9 | 9 | 9 | 9 | 9 | 9 | 9 | 9 |
| 8 | 8 | 8 | 8 | 8 | 8 | 8 | 8 |
| 7 | 7 | 7 | 7 | 7 | 7 | 7 | 7 |
| 6 | 6 | 6 | 6 | 6 | 6 | 6 | 6 |
| 5 | 5 | 5 | 5 | 5 | 5 | 5 | 5 |
| 4 | 4 | 4 | 4 | 4 | 4 | 4 | 4 |
| 3 | 3 | 3 | 3 | 3 | 3 | 3 | 3 |
| 2 | 2 | 2 | 2 | 2 | 2 | 2 | 2 |
| 1 | 1 | 1 | 1 | 1 | 1 | 1 | 1 |
| **1** | **2** | **3** | **4** | **1** | **2** | **3** | **4** |

| PHRASES 1 (1) | PHRASES 1 (2) | PHRASES 1 (3) | PHRASES 1 (4) | PHRASES 2 (1) | PHRASES 2 (2) | PHRASES 2 (3) | PHRASES 2 (4) | BASELINE (1) | PHRASED READING (1) | PHRASED READING (2) | UN-PHRASED READING (1) | UN-PHRASED READING (2) |
|---|---|---|---|---|---|---|---|---|---|---|---|---|
| 50 | 50 | 50 | 50 | 50 | 50 | 50 | 50 | **248** | **248** | **248** | **248** | **248** |
| 49 | 49 | 49 | 49 | 49 | 49 | 49 | 49 | 245 | 245 | 245 | 245 | 245 |
| 48 | 48 | 48 | 48 | 48 | 48 | 48 | 48 | 240 | 240 | 240 | 240 | 240 |
| 47 | 47 | 47 | 47 | 47 | 47 | 47 | 47 | 235 | 235 | 235 | 235 | 235 |
| 46 | 46 | 46 | 46 | 46 | 46 | 46 | 46 | 230 | 230 | 230 | 230 | 230 |
| 45 | 45 | 45 | 45 | 45 | 45 | 45 | 45 | 225 | 225 | 225 | 225 | 225 |
| 44 | 44 | 44 | 44 | 44 | 44 | 44 | 44 | 220 | 220 | 220 | 220 | 220 |
| 43 | 43 | 43 | 43 | 43 | 43 | 43 | 43 | 215 | 215 | 215 | 215 | 215 |
| 42 | 42 | 42 | 42 | 42 | 42 | 42 | 42 | 210 | 210 | 210 | 210 | 210 |
| 41 | 41 | 41 | 41 | 41 | 41 | 41 | 41 | 205 | 205 | 205 | 205 | 205 |
| 40 | 40 | 40 | 40 | 40 | 40 | 40 | 40 | 200 | 200 | 200 | 200 | 200 |
| 39 | 39 | 39 | 39 | 39 | 39 | 39 | 39 | 195 | 195 | 195 | 195 | 195 |
| 38 | 38 | 38 | 38 | 38 | 38 | 38 | 38 | 190 | 190 | 190 | 190 | 190 |
| 37 | 37 | 37 | 37 | 37 | 37 | 37 | 37 | 185 | 185 | 185 | 185 | 185 |
| 36 | 36 | 36 | 36 | 36 | 36 | 36 | 36 | 180 | 180 | 180 | 180 | 180 |
| 35 | 35 | 35 | 35 | 35 | 35 | 35 | 35 | 175 | 175 | 175 | 175 | 175 |
| 34 | 34 | 34 | 34 | 34 | 34 | 34 | 34 | 170 | 170 | 170 | 170 | 170 |
| 33 | 33 | 33 | 33 | 33 | 33 | 33 | 33 | 165 | 165 | 165 | 165 | 165 |
| 32 | 32 | 32 | 32 | 32 | 32 | 32 | 32 | 160 | 160 | 160 | 160 | 160 |
| 31 | 31 | 31 | 31 | 31 | 31 | 31 | 31 | 155 | 155 | 155 | 155 | 155 |
| 30 | 30 | 30 | 30 | 30 | 30 | 30 | 30 | 150 | 150 | 150 | 150 | 150 |
| 29 | 29 | 29 | 29 | 29 | 29 | 29 | 29 | 145 | 145 | 145 | 145 | 145 |
| 28 | 28 | 28 | 28 | 28 | 28 | 28 | 28 | 140 | 140 | 140 | 140 | 140 |
| 27 | 27 | 27 | 27 | 27 | 27 | 27 | 27 | 135 | 135 | 135 | 135 | 135 |
| 26 | 26 | 26 | 26 | 26 | 26 | 26 | 26 | 130 | 130 | 130 | 130 | 130 |
| 25 | 25 | 25 | 25 | 25 | 25 | 25 | 25 | 125 | 125 | 125 | 125 | 125 |
| 24 | 24 | 24 | 24 | 24 | 24 | 24 | 24 | 120 | 120 | 120 | 120 | 120 |
| 23 | 23 | 23 | 23 | 23 | 23 | 23 | 23 | 115 | 115 | 115 | 115 | 115 |
| 22 | 22 | 22 | 22 | 22 | 22 | 22 | 22 | 110 | 110 | 110 | 110 | 110 |
| 21 | 21 | 21 | 21 | 21 | 21 | 21 | 21 | 105 | 105 | 105 | 105 | 105 |
| 20 | 20 | 20 | 20 | 20 | 20 | 20 | 20 | 100 | 100 | 100 | 100 | 100 |
| 19 | 19 | 19 | 19 | 19 | 19 | 19 | 19 | 95 | 95 | 95 | 95 | 95 |
| 18 | 18 | 18 | 18 | 18 | 18 | 18 | 18 | 90 | 90 | 90 | 90 | 90 |
| 17 | 17 | 17 | 17 | 17 | 17 | 17 | 17 | 85 | 85 | 85 | 85 | 85 |
| 16 | 16 | 16 | 16 | 16 | 16 | 16 | 16 | 80 | 80 | 80 | 80 | 80 |
| 15 | 15 | 15 | 15 | 15 | 15 | 15 | 15 | 75 | 75 | 75 | 75 | 75 |
| 14 | 14 | 14 | 14 | 14 | 14 | 14 | 14 | 70 | 70 | 70 | 70 | 70 |
| 13 | 13 | 13 | 13 | 13 | 13 | 13 | 13 | 65 | 65 | 65 | 65 | 65 |
| 12 | 12 | 12 | 12 | 12 | 12 | 12 | 12 | 60 | 60 | 60 | 60 | 60 |
| 11 | 11 | 11 | 11 | 11 | 11 | 11 | 11 | 55 | 55 | 55 | 55 | 55 |
| 10 | 10 | 10 | 10 | 10 | 10 | 10 | 10 | 50 | 50 | 50 | 50 | 50 |
| 9 | 9 | 9 | 9 | 9 | 9 | 9 | 9 | 45 | 45 | 45 | 45 | 45 |
| 8 | 8 | 8 | 8 | 8 | 8 | 8 | 8 | 40 | 40 | 40 | 40 | 40 |
| 7 | 7 | 7 | 7 | 7 | 7 | 7 | 7 | 35 | 35 | 35 | 35 | 35 |
| 6 | 6 | 6 | 6 | 6 | 6 | 6 | 6 | 30 | 30 | 30 | 30 | 30 |
| 5 | 5 | 5 | 5 | 5 | 5 | 5 | 5 | 25 | 25 | 25 | 25 | 25 |
| 4 | 4 | 4 | 4 | 4 | 4 | 4 | 4 | 20 | 20 | 20 | 20 | 20 |
| 3 | 3 | 3 | 3 | 3 | 3 | 3 | 3 | 15 | 15 | 15 | 15 | 15 |
| 2 | 2 | 2 | 2 | 2 | 2 | 2 | 2 | 10 | 10 | 10 | 10 | 10 |
| 1 | 1 | 1 | 1 | 1 | 1 | 1 | 1 | 5 | 5 | 5 | 5 | 5 |
| **1** | **2** | **3** | **4** | **1** | **2** | **3** | **4** | **1** | **1** | **2** | **1** | **2** |

**Split Cliffs Hike**

| | | | | |
|---|---|---|---|---|
| split | strap | jump | cliffs | tempt |
| hills | spring | snack | wind | kept |
| blasts | plants | drink | swept | gets |
| trash | splash | things | kids | dump |
| strong | small | pick | cold | cross |

WORDS 2

| | | | | |
|---|---|---|---|---|
| they | one | from | some | see |
| are | two | water | into | who |
| to | could | you | what | first |
| have | would | out | day | other |
| do | and | by | or | both |

STORY **5**

the Split Cliffs

a spring day

fun to jump

bring some things

to dump trash

in the hills

some kids splash

cross the water

the wind blasts

helps to strap

from rock to rock

did not find

kids just jump

a back pack

will tempt you

dust is swept off

are split by a river

not right to dump trash

could go on a hike

that is why they are

there is a strong wind

the wind blasts the sand

to go to Split Cliffs

should bring some things

jump up on the big rocks

splash in the cold river

# Split Cliffs Hike

If you could go on a hike along the Split Cliffs, what would you see? The first things that you would see are the tall cliffs that are split by a river. That is why they are called Split Cliffs. Next you would see plants along the hills. There are so, so many of them! In the spring, most of them are pink, but some of the others are red. There are lots of rocks – both big and small. It is fun to jump up on the big rocks. Some kids splash in the cold river, but other kids just jump from rock to rock to cross the water. Along the cliffs, the wind blasts the sand and dust. The dust is swept off the cliffs into the river bed.

If you go on a hike, you should bring some things with you. When there is a strong wind, it gets cold on Split Cliffs, so bring a jacket. It helps to strap a back pack on with a snack and a drink or two.

It is sad when you see trash at Split Cliffs. It is not right to dump trash when you are on a hike. If you are out on the cliffs or in the hills and you see some trash, pick it up. That is one thing that you can do to help.

I think that this will tempt you to go to Split Cliffs. It is best on a spring day. Have fun!

# Split Cliffs Hike

If you could go on a hike along the Split Cliffs, what would you see? The first things that you would see are the tall cliffs that are split by a river. That is why they are called Split Cliffs. Next you would see plants along the hills. There are so, so many of them! In the spring, most of them are pink, but some of the others are red. There are lots of rocks – both big and small. It is fun to jump up on the big rocks. Some kids splash in the cold river, but other kids just jump from rock to rock to cross the water. Along the cliffs, the wind blasts the sand and dust. The dust is swept off the cliffs into the river bed.

If you go on a hike, you should bring some things with you. When there is a strong wind, it gets cold on Split Cliffs, so bring a jacket. It helps to strap a back pack on with a snack and a drink or two.

It is sad when you see trash at Split Cliffs. It is not right to dump trash when you are on a hike. If you are out on the cliffs or in the hills and you see some trash, pick it up. That is one thing that you can do to help.

I think that this will tempt you to go to Split Cliffs. It is best on a spring day. Have fun!

# NOTES

# NOTES

# NOTES

# NOTES

# NOTES

**Wilson Fluency®**

www.wilsonlanguage.com

(800) 899-8454

ISBN 978-1-56778-317-9

9 781567 783179

ITEM # WFBR2